Religions of the World

Your Great Big Grab Bag of Useless Helpful Tidbits

Michael P. Clutton

Published by Michael Clutton, 2024.

While every precaution has been taken in the preparation of this book, the publisher assumes no responsibility for errors or omissions, or for damages resulting from the use of the information contained herein.

RELIGIONS OF THE WORLD

First edition. June 15, 2024.

ISBN: 979-8227327147

Written by Michael P. Clutton.

Table of Contents

In a world where skyscrapers touch the heavens, and our digital footprints span continents in mere seconds, the ancient tug of spirituality remains as profound as ever. Religion, in its myriad forms—from the chanted prayers in the Vatican to the rhythmic drumming in a remote tribal village—continues to shape our lives, laws, and sense of purpose. But what makes these diverse beliefs tick? How do they simultaneously divide and unite us? This book, "Divinely Diverse: An Amusing Journey Through the World's Religions and Pseudo-Religions," sets out to explore these questions with a blend of curiosity and joy, peeling back the layers of dogma to reveal the humanity at the heart of faith.

Religion, often considered a solemn affair, is also ripe with peculiarities and paradoxes. It's these quirks and qualities that "Divinely Diverse" aims to highlight. Through a tapestry of historical anecdotes, little-known facts, and amusing vignettes, we will journey through the vast landscape of spiritual belief systems. From the grandeur of ancient rites to the earnest oddities of modern pseudo-religions, every chapter aims to enlighten as much as it entertains.

This is not a theological treatise nor an exhaustive encyclopedia. Instead, consider it your travel guide to the spiritual world, one that offers both the forest and the trees. Whether you are a devout practitioner, a curious onlooker, or an earnest skeptic, there is something here for you. By the end, perhaps we will not only better understand the beliefs of our neighbors but also appreciate the wonderfully complex tapestry of faith that encompasses human civilization.

So, fasten your seatbelt and prepare for a whirlwind tour of the world's religions and pseudo-religions. We promise to deliver enlightenment and entertainment, with a few surprises along the way!

Chapter 1: The Big Five

The Great Interfaith Mix-up

Imagine the scene: a prestigious global interfaith conference that fosters peace and understanding among the world's major religions, set in the ornate halls of an old European city. The delegates—priests, imams, rabbis, monks, and swamis—arrive with noble intentions. But then, due to a comical mishap involving the mistranslation of the conference schedule from English to multiple languages, an impromptu salsa dance class replaces the Buddhist meditation session, the Christian prayer meeting suddenly features incense and mantras meant for the Hindus, and the Jewish kosher lunch is mistakenly swapped with the Halal spread. Confusion reigns, but everyone is laughing over shared stories of similar faux pas in their practices when the mix-up is sorted. It's a poignant reminder that sometimes, understanding comes best through shared mistakes.

15 Tidbits: Exploring the Core and Curiosities of Christianity, Islam, Hinduism, Buddhism, and Judaism

1. **Christianity: A Global Faith** - With over 2.3 billion adherents, Christianity is the world's largest religion. It began as a small Jewish sect in the Middle East and now spans the globe, influencing art, politics, and law in countless cultures.

2. **Islam: The Faith of Submission** - Islam, which means 'submission to the will of God,' boasts nearly 1.8 billion followers. It's not just a religion but a complete way of

life, influencing legal systems and daily practices from Morocco to Indonesia.

3. **Hinduism: A Divine Spectrum**—Hinduism, one of the oldest religions in the world, has a complex pantheon of gods and goddesses. It's said that 330 million deities embody various aspects of life and the universe.

4. **Buddhism: The Middle Way**—Founded by Siddhartha Gautama, or the Buddha, in the 5th century BCE, Buddhism teaches the pursuit of enlightenment through the middle path, avoiding severe asceticism and worldly indulgence.

5. **Judaism: The Covenant People** - Judaism is more than a religion; it's a covenant between God and the Hebrew people. With its profound emphasis on law, ethics, and holy texts, Judaism forms the spiritual foundation for Christianity and Islam.

6. **Christianity's Impact on the Arts** - From Michelangelo's Sistine Chapel to Handel's "Messiah," Christianity has profoundly influenced Western art, leaving a legacy of breathtaking works that continue to inspire beyond religious contexts.

7. **Islamic Contributions to Science** - During the Golden Age of Islam, Muslim scholars made significant advances in fields like mathematics, astronomy, and medicine, much of which laid the groundwork for the Renaissance.

8. **Hinduism and Reincarnation** - The concept of reincarnation, central to Hindu belief, emphasizes karma and the eternal cycle of life, death, and rebirth,

influencing daily behavior and ethical decision-making.

9. **Buddhist Meditation** - Mindfulness and meditation are core Buddhist practices that focus on developing self-awareness, wisdom, and compassion, now widespread globally in secular contexts.

10. **Jewish Dietary Laws** - Kosher laws govern what can be eaten, how food should be prepared, and with whom one can eat, reflecting Judaism's deep connection between faith, practice, and daily life.

11. **Christianity's Diverse Denominations** - There are over 33,000 denominations of Christianity, each interpreting the Bible and the teachings of Jesus in uniquely nuanced ways.

12. **Islam's Pilgrimage: The Hajj—Every physically and financially able Muslim must perform it** at least once. This pilgrimage to Mecca is one of the largest annual gatherings in the world.

13. **Hindu Festivals** - Festivals like Diwali (the Festival of Lights) and Holi (the Festival of Colors) are celebrated enthusiastically, reflecting Hinduism's rich tradition of mythology, music, dance, and storytelling.

14. **Buddhist Non-Violence** - Buddhism's principle of ahimsa (non-violence) profoundly influences its adherents' attitudes toward all living beings, shaping ethical practices and lifestyle choices.

15. **The Jewish Sabbath** - Shabbat, or the Jewish Sabbath, is a day of rest and spiritual enrichment observed from Friday evening to Saturday evening, underscoring the importance of rest in Jewish life.

Great Big Grab Bag of Useless Helpful Tidbits

1. **Saintly Figures** - Christianity officially recognizes over 10,000 saints, patronizing different aspects of life and offering protection in specific areas.
2. **Quranic Preservation**—The Quran has been memorized cover to cover by millions, known as Hafiz, and is regarded as one of the most memorized books in the world.
3. **Multiplicity of Hindu Gods** - Despite the common claim of 330 million Hindu gods, scholars argue that this number metaphorically represents the infinite aspects of the divine rather than a literal count.

Chapter 2: The Eastern Philosophies

The Misunderstood Philosopher

Picture an ancient philosopher, his wisdom spreading far and wide but not quite in the way he intended. In 7th-century China, enthusiastic yet slightly baffled by the original texts, a well-meaning translator turned profound philosophical insights into what sounded remarkably like advice for brewing herbal teas. This curious error went unnoticed for centuries, delighting and confusing scholars who debated the more profound metaphysical implications of "steeping one's spirit" and "balancing the essence of flavor." Such misinterpretations, while humorous, beautifully illustrate the challenges and charms of translating Eastern philosophies to a global audience.

15 Tidbits: Exploring Taoism, Shinto, Confucianism, and More

1. **Taoism: The Way of Nature** - Taoism advocates living in harmony with the Tao, an indefinable force that flows through all life. Its texts, the "Tao Te Ching," by the mystic Laozi, teach simplicity and spontaneity.

2. **Shinto: The Spirit of Japan** - Rooted in ancient Japanese folklore, Shinto practices involve kami worship, spirits associated with natural elements and ancestors. It emphasizes purity, community involvement, and ritual respect for nature.

3. **Confucianism: A Blueprint for Society -** Confucianism isn't just a religion but a philosophical

system that has shaped East Asian societies. It espouses virtues like respect for authority, filial piety, and the importance of education.

4. **Taoist Alchemy and Immortality**—One of the more esoteric aspects of Taoism is the pursuit of physical immortality through alchemy, which involves intricate rituals and medicinal concoctions.

5. **Shinto Festivals** - Shintoism celebrates numerous matsuri (festivals) and vibrant ceremonies, often involving processions, traditional music, and dance, connecting the community to its ancient roots.

6. **The Analects of Confucius**—The primary text of Confucianism, The Analects, is a collection of sayings and ideas attributed to the Chinese philosopher Confucius and his disciples. It focuses on morality and politics.

7. **Zen Buddhism: Meditation and Mindfulness**—Although Zen stems from Buddhism, it emphasizes meditation (zazen) and direct insights rather than scripture study, which it considers secondary.

8. **Art in Taoism** - Taoist philosophy profoundly influences Chinese art, encouraging spontaneous expressions of the natural world, as seen in the fluid brush strokes of ink painting.

9. **Shinto and Japanese Imperial Ceremony** - Shinto rituals are integral to numerous imperial ceremonies in Japan, including enthronement rituals, reflecting the sacred nature of the emperor.

10. **Confucianism and Modern Business** - Confucian

values like hierarchy, respect, and discipline heavily influence corporate cultures throughout Asia, notably in South Korea and Japan.

11. **Taoist Martial Arts** - Taoism significantly impacts martial arts like Tai Chi, which combines self-defense techniques with meditation and breath control, aiming for physical and spiritual harmony.

12. **Shinto Shrines** - Japan houses over 80,000 Shinto shrines, from grand structures like Ise Jingu to tiny roadside spaces, each uniquely venerating local kami.

13. **Confucian Rites** - Confucianism heavily emphasizes rituals (Li) concerning births, marriages, and deaths, designed to reinforce family and social harmony.

14. **The Global Influence of Zen** - Zen Buddhism has a global audience, appealing to those seeking mindfulness and simplicity in an increasingly complex world.

15. **Philosophical Debate in Confucianism** - Historically, Confucian academies were hubs for vigorous philosophical debates that shaped governance and moral codes throughout East Asia.

Great Big Grab Bag of Useless Helpful Tidbits

1. **Taoist Texts** - The "Tao Te Ching" has been translated into over 250 languages, making it one of the most translated works in the world after the Bible and the Quran.

2. **Shinto Shrines** - Japan has approximately 80,000

registered Shinto shrines, but the number of unregistered and small family altars could be much higher.

3. **Confucius's Misquoted Sayings** - Scholars estimate that over half of the famous quotes attributed to Confucius in the Western world are either misquoted or fabricated.

Chapter 3: The New Age and Pseudo-Religions

The First Modern-Day Witch Gathering

Imagine the scene: a lush forest clearing in 1950s England, as a group of modern-day witches attempts to coordinate what they hope to be a historic gathering. The agenda includes casting circles, invoking the elements, and a spirited debate over which moon phase is best for prosperity spells. However, logistics turn nightmarish when two attendees accidentally bring identical cauldrons, leading to a heated discussion about which is genuinely ancient and which is a mere replica from a local garden center. The comedic misunderstandings culminate in a potluck dinner where everyone is wary of the "mystery" stew. Though fraught with mishaps, this inaugural witch meetup marks a pivotal moment in reviving pagan practices and sets the stage for the growth of Wicca and similar movements.

15 Tidbits: Exploring Scientology, Wicca, Raelism, and Other Modern Movements

1. **Scientology: The Hollywood Religion** - Founded by L. Ron Hubbard in 1952, Scientology is a religion that intriguingly blends science fiction elements with psychotherapy techniques, creating a unique and complex belief system. The religion's foundational text, "Dianetics: The Modern Science of Mental Health," posits that human suffering stems from repressed memories of past traumas, known as "engrams," which

can be cleared through a process called "auditing." Auditing sessions, often conducted using an E-meter device, are meant to help individuals achieve a transparent state, free from the influence of these engrams. Scientology is also known for its shroud of secrecy and appeal to celebrities, adding to its mystique and attracting scrutiny. The allure for many in the entertainment industry can be attributed to the religion's focus on personal development, communication skills, and mental clarity—qualities that resonate deeply with those whose careers depend on public performance and persona management.

2. **Wicca: More Than Just Magic** - Wicca is a modern pagan witchcraft religion first brought to public attention in the 1950s by Gerald Gardner, a British civil servant who claimed to have been initiated into a New Forest coven. The religion emphasizes a profound connection to nature, viewing it as a manifestation of the divine and a direct source of spiritual insight. Wiccans practice magic, often focusing on healing, love, and natural harmony, and their rituals are typically aligned with the phases of the moon and the natural seasons. Central to Wiccan belief is the worship of both a God and a Goddess, representing a dualistic view of the universe encompassing both male and female aspects. This structure aims to balance and honor the contributions of both genders to life's cyclical nature and spiritual growth.

3. **Raelism: The UFO Religion** - Established in 1974 by Claude Vorilhon, known as Rael, Raelism involves

believing in intelligent extraterrestrial life that supposedly created humanity using advanced technology.

4. **Wiccan Rede and Ethics** - The core ethical statement of Wicca is the Wiccan Rede: "An it harm none, do what ye will," promoting freedom as long as it harms no one, including nature.

5. **Scientology's Auditing Process**—A central practice in Scientology, auditing involves a one-on-one session with an E-meter, believed to measure mental masses and energies.

6. **Neo-Druidism: Ancient Beliefs and Modern Practices** - Neo-Druidism revives ancient Celtic priesthood in a modern context, focusing on the worship of nature, poetry, and the arts.

7. **Raelism and Cloning Claims** - Raelism gained international attention in 2002 when a company linked to the movement claimed to have cloned the first human being, which was never verified.

8. **Wicca and Environmentalism**—Many Wiccans are involved in environmental causes. They view the Earth as sacred and to be protected, reflecting their belief in the interconnectedness of all life.

9. **The Resurgence of Astrology** - Astrology has recently seen a significant resurgence, particularly among celebrities and young adults. Often considered a form of entertainment rather than a severe religious practice, astrology offers personal insights and guidance through the positions of celestial bodies. Celebrities frequently share their astrological readings on social

media, enhancing their popularity and integrating them into daily conversations about personal and professional decision-making. This trend underscores a growing cultural shift towards incorporating mystical and esoteric practices into mainstream lifestyles.

10. **Public Perception of Pseudo-Religions** - Movements like Scientology and Raelism often face skepticism and controversy, impacting their reception and the legal treatment they receive worldwide.

11. **Wiccan Holidays: The Wheel of the Year** - Wiccans celebrate eight significant holidays or Sabbats, which mark the changing seasons and cycles of nature, including Samhain, Beltane, and Yule.

12. **Scientology's Expansive Real Estate Portfolio** - Scientology boasts a significant global presence, including landmark buildings in major cities for worship and recruitment.

13. **Raelism's Embassy for Extraterrestrials**—One of Raelism's goals is to construct an embassy to welcome extraterrestrials back to Earth, which is proposed to be built in Jerusalem.

14. **Growing Popularity of Modern Paganism** - The number of people identifying with modern pagan religions, including Wicca and Neo-Druidism, has steadily grown, reflecting a broader trend of seeking spirituality outside traditional frameworks.

15. **Freedom of Religion and New Movements** - Despite controversy, movements like Scientology are protected under laws guaranteeing freedom of religion, a testament to many countries' broad interpretation of

religious rights.

Great Big Grab Bag of Useless Helpful Tidbits

1. **Global Scientology Membership Estimates**—According to independent reports, Estimates of Scientology's membership vary widely, from several hundred thousand claimed by the Church to as few as several tens of thousands.
2. **Raelism's Official Alien Landing Sites** - Raelism has designated several sites worldwide as official landing spots for extraterrestrials, with symbols visible from the air.
3. **Wiccan Practitioners' Increase** - According to religious surveys, the number of self-identified Wiccans in the United States has sharply increased, from around 8,000 in 1990 to over 340,000 by 2008.

Chapter 4: The Psychological Underpinnings of Belief in the Divine

Throughout history, most human societies have developed some form of belief in deities or a higher power, a phenomenon that transcends geographic, cultural, and temporal boundaries. This near-universal aspect of human culture points to a deep psychological underpinning: the intrinsic human need to believe in something greater than oneself. Psychologists and anthropologists have long studied this aspect of human behavior, uncovering several key reasons why this tendency towards spirituality and worship is so prevalent.

Firstly, belief in a higher power or divine entity provides a powerful psychological anchor in times of uncertainty and distress. It offers comfort and reassurance, creating a sense of stability and order in what might otherwise seem a chaotic existence. This can be particularly significant during life's trials and tribulations, where believing in a benevolent force can provide hope and the strength to persevere. Such beliefs often enhance an individual's resilience against life's stresses, suggesting a coping mechanism deeply embedded in the human psyche.

Secondly, worship and spiritual practices fulfill a communal need, fostering social cohesion and collective identity among followers. Participating in religious rituals and ceremonies can strengthen bonds within a community, creating a shared experience and collective narrative that reinforces social norms and moral values. This communal aspect can be a glue that holds societies together, promoting social harmony and mutual support.

Moreover, the concept of a higher power often serves as a moral compass, guiding individuals in ethical conduct and decision-making. Many religions provide a framework of moral and ethical guidelines that help shape the behaviors and interactions of their adherents. This regulates individual behavior and provides a common set of standards by which a community can live harmoniously. The fear of divine retribution or the promise of an afterlife reward plays a significant role in encouraging ethical behavior and deterring misconduct.

Furthermore, the human curiosity about life's big questions—Why are we here? What happens after death? Is there more to the universe than meets the eye?—fuels religious and spiritual inquiry. Deities or spiritual beliefs explain these existential questions, satisfying the human quest for knowledge and understanding. This aspect of belief systems addresses the cognitive dimension of our psychology, where understanding and meaning-making are fundamental needs.

The psychological need to believe in a deity or something greater reflects a complex interplay of emotional comfort, social cohesion, moral guidance, and existential curiosity. These needs have driven the formation and evolution of religions across time and cultures, highlighting spirituality and worship's profound and enduring role in human life.

Chapter 5: Indigenous and Tribal Religions

A Comical Cultural Misstep

Imagine a well-meaning Western anthropologist arriving in a remote Amazonian village, eager to document and participate in local religious practices. Intent on making a good impression, he dons what he believes to be traditional ceremonial attire, only to discover—to the amused laughter of the local tribe—that he has inadvertently dressed himself in women's ritual garments, a mix-up due to his limited understanding of the local language and customs. Far from being a setback, this hilarious start to his visit breaks the ice and leads to deeper discussions and insights about the tribe's spiritual life, showcasing the importance of humility and humor in cross-cultural exchanges.

15 Tidbits: Exploring Native American Spirituality, African Traditional Religions, Aboriginal Australian Beliefs, and More

1. **Native American Spirituality: Connection with Nature** - Native American religions are deeply intertwined with the land and nature, with each tribe expressing a unique spiritual connection to their environment. Practices and beliefs vary significantly among tribes, but common elements include animism, ritual dances, and using sacred objects like totems. Animism, a belief central to these religions, posits that all aspects of nature—plants, animals, and even

geographical features—possess a spiritual essence that influences daily life and rituals. Ritual dances serve as expressions of cultural identity and are vital in ceremonies that seek to honor, appease, and communicate with these spirits. Additionally, sacred objects such as totems play crucial roles; crafted from wood and stone, they are revered as physical manifestations of spiritual beings and ancestors, serving as focal points for communal rituals and personal meditation.

2. **African Traditional Religions: Ancestor Worship** - In many African cultures, ancestors play a central role in religious practice. These religions often involve rituals to honor ancestors, who are believed to influence the living from the spiritual realm.

3. **Aboriginal Australian Dreamtime** - Aboriginal spirituality centers around the Dreamtime, a complex network of stories, symbols, and rituals that describe the creation of the universe and govern the rules of living and social behavior.

4. **Shamanism Across Cultures**—Shamanism appears in various forms worldwide. Generally, it involves a practitioner reaching altered states of consciousness to interact with the spirit world, often for healing or divination purposes.

5. **The Sun Dance: A Sacred Ceremony**—The Sun Dance is a significant ceremony practiced by several North American Plains tribes. It involves dancing, fasting, and, in some traditions, body piercing as a form of sacrifice and spiritual rebirth.

6. **Santería: A Fusion of African and Christian Elements**—Originating among Afro-Cuban communities, Santería blends the Yoruba religion brought by enslaved West Africans with Roman Catholicism. It is characterized by the worship of Orishas, akin to saints.

7. **The Role of Masks in African Rituals** - Masks are vital in many African traditional religions, used during rituals and ceremonies to represent various deities or spirits, facilitating communication between humans and the divine.

8. **Native American Vision Quests**—Vision quests are pivotal spiritual journeys undertaken primarily by young males to seek spiritual guidance or protection from the spirits, marking a transition into adulthood.

9. **Peyote Worship in Native American Church**—The Native American Church incorporates peyote, a hallucinogenic cactus, in its ceremonies. It is regarded as a sacrament that brings healing and spiritual insight.

10. **The Green Corn Ceremony of the Cherokee**—This annual harvest festival is crucial for the Cherokee and other Southeastern tribes. It celebrates the first corn crop's ripening and features dancing, feasting, and ritual renewals of community bonds.

11. **Aboriginal Sacred Sites** - Aboriginal Australians hold certain landscapes, like Uluru and other rock formations, as sacred. These sites are crucial for their spiritual identity and practices.

12. **Animism in Southeast Asia**—Many tribal religions practice animism, believing spirits inhabit living and

non-living entities. This belief influences daily practices and respect for nature.

13. **Hoodoo: African American Spirituality** - Hoodoo is a traditional African American spirituality that combines elements of Congo river basin traditions, Native American herbalism, and European folk magic.

14. **The Vodou Religion of Haiti** blends African animistic practices and Christianity. It is known for its complex spirits (loa) and rituals, which profoundly influence Haitian culture and identity.

15. **Ifá Divination System** - Practiced by the Yoruba and other West African peoples, Ifá involves divination using an intricate system of symbols and chants to communicate with the spiritual world and seek guidance.

Great Big Grab Bag of Useless Helpful Tidbits

1. **Languages and Rituals**—Over 1,000 different languages are spoken by Indigenous groups in the Amazon alone, each associated with unique religious rituals and practices.

2. **Sacred Sites Conservation**—It is estimated that over 100,000 Aboriginal sacred sites exist in Australia, though many are under threat from mining and urban development.

3. **Ceremonial Artifacts Rarity**—Fewer than 200 original Native American Ghost Dance shirts exist today, many held in museums outside their

communities. They symbolize the loss and ongoing efforts for cultural preservation.

Chapter 6: Extinct Religions

The Misinterpreted Artifact

Imagine the puzzled faces of historians when they unearthed what was believed to be a profound religious artifact, only to discover, after decades of speculation and scholarly debate, that it was merely a children's toy. This humorous episode is a gentle reminder of how the sands of time can obscure the true meanings and uses of objects from ancient civilizations, leading to charming but erroneous reconstructions of their cultural and religious practices. Such misunderstandings underscore the challenges in studying extinct religions, where archaeologists and historians must piece together the fragmented remains of long-lost worlds.

15 Tidbits: Exploring the Beliefs and Gods of Ancient Egyptian, Norse, Greek, and Other No-Longer-Practiced Religions

1. **Ancient Egyptian Religion: A Pantheon of Deities** - Ancient Egypt was a civilization deeply immersed in religious practices, where each aspect of life and the cosmos was infused with spirituality. The Egyptians revered a vast pantheon of deities, such as Osiris, the god of the afterlife; Isis, the goddess of magic and motherhood; and Anubis, the jackal-headed god of embalming and the dead. These gods and goddesses were worshipped not only in prominent temples staffed by priests but also central to everyday life and

the overarching cosmology of the Egyptians. Rituals and offerings were made to sustain these deities, who, in return, were believed to maintain the order of the universe and bless the land with fertility and prosperity. The religious culture of Ancient Egypt was thus rich and complex, permeating nearly every aspect of its people's lives, from the grandest temples to the most minor households.

2. **Norse Mythology: The Viking Legacy** - Norse mythology was the backbone of Viking society, shaping their worldview, daily activities, and long-term aspirations. Tales of gods like Odin, the all-seeing father of the gods; Thor, the thunderous protector wielding his hammer; and Loki, the cunning trickster, were more than just stories. They offered models of bravery, strategy, and cunning that influenced Viking warfare and tactics. Moreover, these myths permeated the social structure, reinforcing the values of loyalty and heroism that were vital in Viking explorations and conquests. The gods were considered active participants in the world, guiding and impacting the Vikings' journeys to unknown lands, thus inspiring a culture renowned for its fearless maritime explorations.

3. **Greek Pantheon: Gods of Human Traits** - The ancient Greeks created a complex pantheon of deities who personified human qualities and embodied the forces of nature, shaping the Greek understanding of the world around them. Zeus, the omnipotent king of the gods, ruled the skies and wielded thunder, symbolizing authority and justice. Aphrodite, the

goddess of love and beauty, influenced human relationships and was revered in rituals to foster attraction and romance. This rich tapestry of gods and goddesses, including Poseidon, who commanded the sea, and Athena, who represented wisdom and war strategy, profoundly influenced Greek culture. Their stories, rituals, and symbols permeated every aspect of life, from the personal to the political, teaching values, explaining natural phenomena, and providing a basis for the vibrant mythologies that continue to influence modern culture.

4. **The Mystery Cults of Ancient Greece** - Initiates of these secretive cults, such as those dedicated to Dionysus or Demeter, participated in private rituals and believed in mystical experiences that promised a path to a happier afterlife.

5. **Roman State Religion: Civic Duty and Piety** - The Romans integrated their religious practices with the state, honoring an array of gods through public rituals and festivals that reinforced civic responsibilities and the emperor's authority.

6. **Celtic Druidism: Nature and the Otherworld** - The Druids, priests of the ancient Celts, practiced a religion focused on worshipping nature spirits, the divine nature of trees, and an intricate belief in the Otherworld.

7. **Aztec Sacrifices: Propitiating the Gods**—The Aztecs are infamous for their religious rituals involving human sacrifices, which they believed appeased gods and ensured the continuation of the world.

8. **Mayan Religion: Astronomy and Sacrifice** - The Mayans developed an intricate religion that closely intertwined their advanced knowledge of astronomy with their religious rituals, often culminating in human sacrifices.

9. **Sumerian Religion: The Cradle of Civilization** - Sumerians, one of the earliest civilizations, worshiped a pantheon of gods thought to control every aspect of life and nature, profoundly influencing Mesopotamian culture.

10. **Zoroastrianism: The Battle of Good and Evil** - While not entirely extinct, Zoroastrianism was one of the world's first monotheistic religions, centered around the constant battle between Ahura Mazda (good) and Angra Mainyu (evil).

11. **The Cult of Mithras: A Roman Mystery Religion** - Popular among Roman soldiers, this secretive cult worshipped Mithras, the god of contracts, and was known for its complex initiation rites and symbolism.

12. **Etruscan Religion: Haruspicy and Prophecy** - The Etruscans practiced haruspicy, divining the future from the entrails of sacrificed animals, which profoundly influenced Roman religious practices.

13. **The Phoenician Pantheon: Trade and Deities** - Phoenicians worshiped various gods, like Baal and Astarte, which influenced their maritime ventures and were spread across the Mediterranean through trade.

14. **The Religion of Carthage: Child Sacrifice and Baal Worship** - Historical and archaeological evidence suggests that the Carthaginians practiced child

sacrifice to appease their gods, particularly Baal Hammon.

15. **Hittite Practices: Rituals and Festivals** - The Hittites, an ancient Anatolian people, had a complex system of rituals and festivals that involved multiple gods and goddesses, integral to their societal structure and kingship.

Great Big Grab Bag of Useless Helpful Tidbits

1. **Number of Gods in Norse Pantheon** - Scholars believe that Norse mythology had over 60 distinct gods and goddesses, each associated with specific aspects of life, such as war, fertility, and the sea.

2. **Animal Sacrifices in Ancient Egypt** - It is estimated that over 400,000 animals were sacrificed annually at the height of ancient Egyptian religious practices.

3. **Oldest Recorded Myths** - Some Sumerian myths recorded in cuneiform on clay tablets are among the oldest known religious texts, dating back over 5,000 years.

Chapter 7: The Manipulation of Religious Belief by the Elite

Throughout history, the intricate relationship between religion and power has often been characterized by manipulation and control. Royalty, monarchs, church leaders, and other upper-class members in many civilizations have recognized the psychological and social needs of the populace to believe in something greater than themselves. They have frequently harnessed these beliefs to consolidate and expand their power, sometimes even altering religious doctrines to ensure the populace remained submissive and loyal.

Religion, with its profound influence on the hearts and minds of people, has often been an effective tool for governance. In many societies, the ruling classes endorsed or promoted religious teachings emphasizing virtues like obedience, humility, and contentment with one's societal position. By aligning themselves with the divine—often claiming divine right to rule or portraying themselves as chosen by the gods—monarchs and religious leaders could justify their authority and quell dissent. This divine endorsement discouraged rebellion and fostered a stable, controlled society where questioning the social order could be framed as religious heresy.

Moreover, religious rituals and ceremonies were designed to reinforce this social hierarchy. Grand religious processions and elaborate ceremonies often depicted rulers in close communion with divine figures, visually reinforcing their special status in the cosmic order. The opulence and splendor of these events served to awe the ordinary people, simultaneously deepening their religious faith and allegiance to their rulers.

The elite's manipulation of religious beliefs also extended to the control of knowledge and education. By restricting the interpretation of sacred texts and religious doctrine to a select few, the upper echelons of society could control the narrative. This ensured that theological debates and interpretations of scripture that might undermine the established order were suppressed. In some cases, translations of sacred texts were forbidden, keeping the power of literacy and understanding in the hands of the elite, further entrenching their control.

Additionally, laws and policies were often cloaked in religious language, making it seem that adherence to the law was equivalent to divine command. This tactic bolstered the legitimacy of legal codes and made them seem immutable and sacred beyond human questioning or change.

Of course, this strategic use of religion was not without its critics and opponents. Throughout history, various reform movements have arisen to challenge the entwining of religious dogma with temporal power, advocating for a return to more spiritual or doctrinally pure forms of worship and governance. These movements sometimes gave rise to new forms of religious practice and occasionally even altered the political landscape.

In conclusion, the manipulation of religious beliefs by societal elites highlights a darker aspect of the relationship between religion and power. While fulfilling a need for spiritual guidance and communal cohesion, religion, when intertwined with the ambitions of the powerful, has also been a tool for social control and political stability, often at the cost of spiritual freedom and social justice.

A Few More Interesting Tidbits About Religions of The World

1. **Bible Translations**: The Bible has been translated into 704 languages in its entirety and into 3,384 languages in part. Notable translations include the King James Version (KJV), completed in 1611, and the New International Version (NIV), first published in 1978. These are just two examples among hundreds of versions, each tailored to different linguistic, doctrinal, and cultural contexts.

2. **Daily Prayers in Islam**: Muslims are required to pray five times a day. These prayers are known as Salat and are observed at specific times throughout the day: before sunrise (Fajr), midday after the sun passes its highest (Dhuhr), the late part of the afternoon (Asr), just after sunset (Maghrib), and between sunset and midnight (Isha).

3. **Number of Recognized Religions**: It's challenging to pinpoint an exact number of religions worldwide due to the vast number of belief systems, sects, and denominations. However, some estimates suggest there are roughly 4,300 recognized religions globally. This number includes everything from major world religions to smaller indigenous faiths.

Chapter 8: The Abrahamic Offshoots

The Forgotten Sect

Picture an intriguing episode from history: a group of religious innovators in the Middle East centuries ago attempting to merge elements from Judaism, Christianity, and Islam into a single faith. They intended to foster unity among the followers of these monotheistic religions. Unfortunately, due to linguistic misunderstandings and differing doctrinal interpretations, their efforts led to some comical misapplications of religious practices—like fasting from sunrise to sunset, then immediately breaking it with a giant pork feast. Although their movement never gained mainstream traction, this forgotten sect provides a fascinating glimpse into the creative, albeit sometimes misguided, attempts to bridge religious divides.

15 Tidbits: Exploring Lesser-Known Religions Derived from Judaism, Christianity, and Islam

1. **Druze: A Blend of Abrahamic Beliefs** - Originating in the 11th century in Egypt, the Druze faith incorporates elements from Islam, Judaism, and Christianity but has evolved its unique theological system that emphasizes reincarnation and a mystical connection to the divine.

2. **Baha'i Faith: Unity of All Religions** - Founded in the 19th century in Persia, the Baha'i Faith teaches the unity of all major religions and the belief that all prophets are part of a single progressive revelation,

culminating in the teachings of Baha'u'llah.

3. **Ahmadiyya: A Reformist Movement in Islam**—Established in late 19th-century India, Ahmadiyya emphasizes the peaceful propagation of Islam and believes in Mirza Ghulam Ahmad as the promised Messiah and Mahdi.

4. **Samaritanism: Preserving Ancient Israelite Traditions**—The Samaritans, whose roots trace back to ancient Israel and Judah, continue to practice a form of ancient Israelite religion. They adhere closely to the Pentateuch but differ from mainstream Judaism.

5. **Messianic Judaism: Combining Christian and Jewish Beliefs**—Messianic Judaism believes in Jesus as the Messiah but adheres to Jewish laws and customs, blending elements of both Christianity and Judaism in its practices.

6. **The Rastafari Movement: Afrocentric Biblical Interpretation**—Emerging in 1930s Jamaica, Rastafari focuses on reinterpreting the Bible through an Afrocentric lens, venerating Haile Selassie of Ethiopia as a god figure and emphasizing liberation from oppressive structures.

7. **Alevism: A Distinctive Islamic Sect** - Alevism is practiced predominantly in Turkey and integrates Shia, Sufi, and local Anatolian folk practices into its rituals, distinguishing itself from mainstream Sunni and Shia Islam.

8. **The Coptic Church: Christianity with Egyptian Roots** - The Coptic Orthodox Church of Alexandria is one of the oldest Christian denominations in the

world, maintaining a unique Egyptian identity and ancient Christian traditions not found in other Eastern Orthodox churches.

9. **Karaite Judaism: Rejecting Rabbinic Traditions** - Karaites reject the oral Torah (Talmud) used by Rabbinic Judaism, relying solely on the Hebrew Scriptures for guidance, which leads to distinct religious practices and interpretations.

10. **The Nation of Islam: African American Islamic Movement** - Founded in the early 20th century in the United States, the Nation of Islam focuses on promoting African American empowerment and a distinct interpretation of Islam separate from mainstream Sunni and Shia traditions.

11. **Mandaeism: An Ancient Gnostic Religion** - Mandaeism has survived for thousands of years in Iraq and Iran, practicing a Gnostic faith that emphasizes the importance of baptism and a unique cosmology unrelated to Christian traditions.

12. **Zaidiyyah: A Branch of Shia Islam** - The Zaidis, a branch of Shia Islam, differ in their belief about the Imamate, which they assert should be a matter of lineage and individual merit.

13. **Chabad-Lubavitch: A Hasidic Jewish Dynasty** - This movement focuses on outreach and education, promoting a deeper understanding of Jewish mysticism and maintaining a vibrant community life centered around the teachings of their Rebbes.

14. **Sufism: The Mystical Dimension of Islam**—Sufism seeks a direct personal experience of God through

mystic rituals and the teachings of saints, offering a spiritual path that emphasizes inner purity and God's love.

15. **The Yazidi Faith: Ancient Mesopotamian Roots** - The Yazidis, often misunderstood and persecuted, follow a syncretic religion that combines aspects of ancient Mesopotamian religious traditions, Islam, and Christianity.

Great Big Grab Bag of Useless Helpful Tidbits

1. **Druze Population**—There are about one million Druze worldwide, with significant populations in Syria, Lebanon, and Israel and a growing diaspora.
2. **Baha'i Adherents**—The Baha'i Faith is among the most widespread religions, with over five million followers in virtually every country.
3. **Ahmadiyya in Pakistan** - Pakistan has the largest population of Ahmadi Muslims, estimated at around 4 million, despite facing significant legal and social challenges.

Chapter 9: Religious Festivals and Pilgrimages

Overbooked Sacred Sites

Imagine the bustling scene at one of the world's most revered pilgrimage sites during a significant religious festival. Due to a clerical error, three religious groups have scheduled their sacred pilgrimages on the same day, leading to a humorous yet chaotic mix of processions, chants, and rituals all converging in the same space. Amid the confusion, pilgrims from diverse backgrounds find common ground in shared meals and exchange stories, turning a logistical nightmare into a spontaneous celebration of unity and faith. This amusing convergence highlights the profound human connections that can emerge from the rich tapestry of religious traditions.

15 Tidbits: Exploring Major Religious Festivals and Pilgrimages

1. **Hajj: The Islamic Pilgrimage to Mecca** - Hajj, one of the five pillars of Islam, requires Muslims to make a pilgrimage to Mecca at least once in their lifetime, provided they are physically and financially able. This journey is a profound expression of Islamic faith and unity.

2. **Kumbh Mela: Hinduism's Massive Gathering** - Held every twelve years at one of four holy locations in India, Kumbh Mela is considered the most significant religious gathering in the world, attracting tens of

millions of Hindus who come to bathe in sacred rivers.

3. **Easter: Christianity's Holiest Celebration**—Easter commemorates the resurrection of Jesus Christ and is the most significant event in the Christian liturgical year. It is celebrated with various customs worldwide, from all-night vigils to festive parades.

4. **Yom Kippur: Jewish Day of Atonement** - Yom Kippur, the holiest day in Judaism, involves 25 hours of fasting and intensive prayer. It is a time for reflection, repentance, and seeking forgiveness.

5. **Diwali: Festival of Lights** - This five-day Hindu festival celebrates the victory of light over darkness and good over evil, marked by the lighting of lamps, fireworks, and sharing of sweets.

6. **Camino de Santiago: Christian Pilgrimage in Spain**—This ancient pilgrimage route culminates at the cathedral of Santiago de Compostela, where the apostle Saint James is said to be buried. Pilgrims walk hundreds of miles, reflecting on their lives and faith.

7. **Bodhi Day: Buddhist Celebration of Enlightenment** - In early December, Bodhi Day commemorates the day that Siddhartha Gautama, the historical Buddha, attained enlightenment under a Bodhi tree.

8. **Ramadan: Islamic Month of Fasting** - Ramadan, the ninth month of the Islamic calendar, is observed by Muslims worldwide as a month of fasting, prayer, reflection, and community.

9. **Purim: Jewish Celebration of Deliverance** - Purim commemorates the saving of the Jewish people from

Haman in ancient Persia, as recounted in the Book of Esther, typically celebrated with public readings, costumes, and gift-giving.

10. **Lent: Christian Period of Preparation for Easter**—In Christianity, Lent is a 40-day season of fasting, prayer, and penance, beginning with Ash Wednesday and preparing believers for Easter.

11. **Wesak: Buddhist New Year** - Wesak, also known as Vesak, Buddha Purnima, and Buddha Day, celebrates the birth, enlightenment, and death of Buddha in one day, observed with much reverence in Buddhist communities around the world.

12. **Sukkot: Jewish Festival of Tabernacles**—Sukkot commemorates the forty years of Israelite wandering in the desert and is celebrated by building and dwelling in temporary shelters, a reminder of the fragility of life.

13. **The Arbaeen Pilgrimage: One of the Largest Annual Gatherings** - The Arbaeen Pilgrimage to Karbala, Iraq, commemorates the martyrdom of Hussein, the grandson of Prophet Muhammad, attracting millions of Shia Muslims.

14. **Pchum Ben: Cambodian Ancestor Day** - During this 15-day Buddhist festival, Cambodians pay respects to their ancestors up to seven generations back, involving offerings at temples and rituals to comfort the spirits of the deceased.

15. **Thaipusam: Tamil Hindu Festival** - Dedicated to the Hindu deity Murugan, Thaipusam is celebrated with a procession involving devotional acts such as carrying kavadis, which are burdens such as pots of milk or

elaborate structures attached to the body.

Great Big Grab Bag of Useless Helpful Tidbits

1. **Attendance at Kumbh Mela** - The 2013 Kumbh Mela in Allahabad, India, drew an estimated 120 million visitors over 55 days, making it one of the largest peaceful gatherings in human history.
2. **Camino de Santiago Pilgrims**—Over 300,000 pilgrims complete the Camino de Santiago each year, walking an average of about 780 kilometers to reach the shrine.
3. **Ramadan Observance**—Over 1.8 billion Muslims observe Ramadan, making it one of the most widely practiced religious rituals worldwide.

Chapter 10: Sacred Texts and Divine Words

The Lost Translation

In a comical twist from the annals of religious history, a mistranslated scripture once led a small sect to adopt highly unconventional practices—such as using lemon cakes as sacred offerings during solemn rituals, believing they were fulfilling a divine command. This misinterpretation, while humorous, sheds light on the profound impact that holy texts can have on religious practices and the importance of accurate translation and interpretation. It serves as a whimsical reminder of the challenges in conveying spiritual truths across different languages and cultures.

15 Tidbits: Exploring the Role and Content of Sacred Texts

1. **The Bible: Christianity's Foundation** - The Bible, composed of the Old and New Testaments, is Christians' spiritual and moral foundation globally. It encompasses a rich collection of historical narratives, poetic writings, prophetic utterances, and doctrinal epistles that narrate the human relationship with the divine, the moral framework to live by, and the salvation history central to Christian belief. This sacred compilation influences not only the personal lives of believers but also shapes church doctrines and practices. It provides narratives that help followers understand and interpret the presence and actions of

God in human history and offers teachings that guide the moral and ethical decisions of its adherents.

Translated into over 3,000 languages, the Bible holds the record for the most translated book in the world, reflecting its extensive reach and universal relevance. This broad dissemination ensures that its teachings are accessible to a diverse global audience, promoting a profound impact on cultural and societal norms across continents. Each translation involves careful consideration to maintain the text's integrity while making it understandable in different cultural and linguistic contexts. This extensive translation effort underscores the Bible's role in fostering an inclusive religious community bound by shared teachings and values, regardless of geographical and cultural boundaries.

1. **The Quran: Islam's Holy Scripture** - The Quran, central to the Islamic faith, is revered as the literal word of God (Allah), revealed to the Prophet Muhammad over approximately 23 years. Muslims believe that through the Quran, Allah communicated his will to humanity, guiding people on how to lead a life that is pleasing to Him and beneficial to society. The text covers many topics, including morality, worship, law, and personal conduct. It is the ultimate authority in religious matters and legal and societal norms within Islamic cultures. Its verses are recited in daily prayers and form the foundation for Islamic

theology, law, and ethics.

Preserving the Quran's original Arabic text is a matter of profound religious importance, as it is thought to hold the precise words spoken by God. Millions of Muslims worldwide strive to memorize the entire Quran, a practice known as Hifz, which is seen as both a way of worshiping and a means of preserving the sacred text across generations. Those who succeed are respected greatly and often play leading roles in community and religious life. This deep engagement with the text not only underscores its religious significance but ensures its influence permeates daily life, shaping the actions and decisions of individuals in myriad ways. This central role of the Quran in Islamic traditions highlights its profound impact on personal lives and the broader community throughout the Islamic world.

1. **The Vedas: Hinduism's Ancient Scriptures** - The Vedas are a collection of texts that form Hinduism's theological and philosophical foundation. Written in Sanskrit, they include hymns, chants, philosophies, rituals, and poems.

2. **The Tripitaka: Buddhist Sacred Texts** - Comprising the Sutta Pitaka, the Vinaya Pitaka, and the Abhidhamma Pitaka, the Tripitaka details the Buddha's teachings and rules for monastic life, playing a central role in Theravada Buddhism.

3. **The Torah: Judaism's Core Text** - The Torah,

consisting of the first five books of the Hebrew Bible, is the primary document of Judaism, containing laws, teachings, and stories that shape Jewish identity and practices.

4. **The Book of Mormon: Latter-Day Saints' Scripture** - The Book of Mormon holds a distinctive place within the Church of Jesus Christ of Latter-Day Saints as a sacred text considered another testament of Jesus Christ, alongside the Bible. It is believed to be a historical and spiritual record of the peoples of the ancient Americas, chronicling their civilizations, wars, migrations, and spiritual revelations from God. Complementing the Bible, the Book of Mormon introduces additional teachings and revelations deemed highly relevant for contemporary followers. It elaborates on doctrines concerning the nature of Christ, redemption, and the conduct of life expected of believers, enriching and expanding the doctrinal framework established by the Bible. For members of the Latter-Day Saint movement, this text serves as a spiritual guide and a confirmatory witness of the divine mission and resurrection of Jesus Christ, integrating these narratives into a broader Christian theology.

5. **The Guru Granth Sahib: Sikhism's Eternal Guru** - The Guru Granth Sahib is not only a sacred scripture but also the eternal spiritual guide in Sikhism, containing hymns and poetry that reflect the teachings of the Sikh Gurus.

6. **The Tao Te Ching: Taoism's Fundamental Text** - This foundational Taoist text, attributed to Laozi, is a

series of meditations on the nature of the Tao and how to live in harmony with the universe.

7. **The Avesta: Zoroastrianism's Sacred Book**—The Avesta contains the holy writings of Zoroastrianism, including the Gathas, hymns believed to have been composed by Zoroaster himself. It is central to Zoroastrian worship and doctrine.

8. **The Talmud: Judaism's Record of Rabbinic Discussions** - The Talmud expands upon the Torah's teachings with detailed discussions and interpretations by rabbis over centuries, influencing all aspects of Jewish law and life.

9. **The Hadith: Islam's Written Traditions**—The Hadith, a collection of Prophet Muhammad's sayings and actions, complements the Quran by guiding practices not explicitly covered in the holy text.

10. **The Book of Shadows: Wiccan Sacred Text** - The Book of Shadows is a deeply personal and unique element of Wiccan practice, serving as an individual's private journal where they document their specific spells, rituals, and magical recipes. Unlike religious texts that are standardized across a faith, each Book of Shadows is distinct and tailored to reflect the particular path and experiences of the practitioner. This customization allows Wiccans to record not only spells and magical insights but also personal reflections and learnings, making each book reflect the practitioner's journey through the craft. The eclectic nature of these books mirrors the diversity within Wicca itself, accommodating a wide range of beliefs

and practices that resonate personally with each practitioner. A personal journal, not standardized, is used by Wiccans to record spells, rituals, and magical recipes, reflecting the eclectic and individual nature of their practices.

11. **The Upanishads: Philosophical Underpinnings of Hinduism** - Part of the Vedas, the Upanishads explore the concepts of the soul (Atman) and the universe (Brahman), offering profound insights into spirituality and ethics.

12. **The Diamond Sutra: Buddhism's Wisdom Texts** - One of the oldest known printed books, the Diamond Sutra is revered in Mahayana Buddhism for its teachings on non-attachment and the perception of reality.

13. **The Enuma Elish: Mesopotamian Creation Epic** - The Enuma Elish, an ancient Babylonian text, details the creation of the world and the rise of the god Marduk, serving as a religious and cultural foundation for ancient Mesopotamian civilization.

Great Big Grab Bag of Useless Helpful Tidbits

1. **Translations of the Bible** - The Bible is the most translated document globally, available fully in 704 languages and partially in 2,932 languages as of 2021.

2. **Memorization of the Quran** - Over 10 million people globally have memorized the Quran, a practice known as Hafiz, which is considered a high honor and

spiritual achievement in Islam.

3. **Ancient Copies of the Vedas** - Despite their ancient origins, the earliest surviving copies of the Vedas date back to only around 500 BC due to the oral tradition of Vedic teachings being passed down before being written.

Chapter 11: Controversial and Taboo Practices

Historical Bans and Bizarre Beliefs

Imagine the confusion and dismay when a deeply-held religious practice, once considered sacred and indispensable within a community, suddenly becomes outlawed by external authorities unfamiliar with its cultural significance. From the ancient Roman prohibitions against the Druids' holy rites to modern laws against animal sacrifices in certain religions, the history of religious practice is riddled with moments of cultural clash and misunderstanding. Such incidents highlight the delicate balance between respecting religious freedom and addressing broader societal concerns, often leading to heated debates and legal battles over acceptable religious expression.

15 Tidbits: Insight into Controversial or Misunderstood Religious Practices

1. **Animal Sacrifice in Santería** - Often misunderstood by outsiders, animal sacrifice in Santería is a profound expression of faith, intended to honor saints and invoke their favor, rooted in West African Yoruba traditions.

2. **Speaking in Tongues in Pentecostal Christianity** - Known as glossolalia, speaking in tongues is considered a sign of divine presence and spiritual blessing within Pentecostal communities. However, it has been met with skepticism and controversy in broader society.

3. **Sati in Hinduism** - Historically, Sati involved a widow voluntarily immolating herself on her husband's funeral pyre, a practice now banned due to its violent implications and the evolving understanding of women's rights within and outside the community.

4. **Ritual Fasting in Jainism**—Some Jain monks and laypersons practice extreme ritual fasting, sometimes leading to death, as a form of spiritual cleansing and detachment from the physical world, sparking debates about religious freedom versus health.

5. **Circumcision in Judaism and Islam** - While circumcision is a covenantal rite in both Judaism and Islam, signifying a lifelong commitment to faith, it has faced modern scrutiny over medical ethics and children's rights.

6. **Sky Burials in Tibetan Buddhism** - In Tibetan Buddhism and some Mongolian traditions, sky burials involve leaving the deceased exposed to the elements and carrion birds, a practice aimed at returning the body to nature but considered taboo by many.

7. **Snake Handling in Certain Christian Sects** - Some small Christian denominations in the United States practice snake handling as evidence of faith and divine protection, leading to legal issues and public safety concerns.

8. **Self-flagellation in Shiite Islam** - During the holy month of Muharram, some Shiite Muslims practice self-flagellation to mourn the martyrdom of Hussein. This practice has sparked internal and external debates about the physical expression of faith.

9. **Witch Trials in Early Modern Europe** - The witch trials were a dark chapter in European history where thousands, mostly women, were executed under accusations of witchcraft, reflecting deep-seated fears and misunderstandings about non-conformist practices.

10. **Thaipusam Body Piercing**—The Hindu festival of Thaipusam involves devotees performing body piercing as a demonstration of faith and penance, practices that can appear extreme to non-adherents.

11. **Cannabis Use in Rastafarianism** - The ceremonial use of cannabis in Rastafarian practices, considered a sacrament for meditation and spiritual insight, clashes with anti-drug laws in many countries.

12. **Foot Binding in Chinese Folk Religion**—Once considered a mark of beauty and status, foot binding in China was physically damaging and reflected broader issues of gender inequality.

13. **Exorcism in Various Religions** - Exorcism, intended to cast out spirits or demons from individuals, while still practiced in many religions, often faces criticism from mental health professionals who caution against misidentifying psychological issues as spiritual afflictions.

14. **Polygamy in Fundamentalist Mormonism** - Polygamy, practiced by some fundamentalist offshoots of mainstream Mormonism, continues to be a subject of legal and ethical debate, particularly in the United States.

15. **Human Sacrifice in Ancient Cultures** - While largely

extinct, human sacrifice in ancient cultures, such as the Aztecs and Maya, remains one of the most controversial religious practices in historical discourse.

Great Big Grab Bag of Useless Helpful Tidbits

1. **Legal Status of Animal Sacrifice**—In 1993, the Supreme Court ruled that animal sacrifice during religious ceremonies is protected under the First Amendment, following a case involving Santería rituals in Florida.

2. **Incidents of Snake Bites in Religious Ceremonies** - Statistics show that over the past 100 years, there have been more than 100 documented deaths related to snake handling in religious practices in the United States.

3. **Global Decline of Female Genital Mutilation/ Cutting** - Though not tied to a single religion and more cultural, the practice has seen a global decline due to extensive human rights campaigns, with a 30% decrease in prevalence over the past three decades.

Chapter 12: Grab a Bag of Divine Trivia

Quirky Religious Facts Unveiled

Embark on a light-hearted exploration into the quirkiest corners of religious practices and beliefs across the globe. From the ancient Egyptians' use of beetles as symbols of resurrection to modern-day church groups holding services in virtual reality settings, religion has always had its share of oddities. These tidbits entertain and offer a glimpse into how humans express and experience their spirituality. This chapter is a delightful collection of the strange, surprising, and sometimes downright bizarre elements within various religious traditions.

Great Big Grab Bag of Pointless Trivia

1. **Holy Smoke!** - Did you know that in Sweden, there is a church that conducts a heavy metal mass? This unique blend of loud guitars and traditional liturgy aims to attract younger congregants, proving that worship can indeed come with a backbeat.
2. **Sanctified Saloons** - In the American Wild West, it wasn't uncommon for saloons to double as places of worship on Sundays, a practical solution in towns where buildings were scarce and the spirit needed uplifting in more ways than one.
3. **The Great Beer Flood of London**—In 1814, a brewery accident in London caused a massive beer vat to burst, unleashing a tidal wave of ale that flooded

streets and even demolished homes. The event was deemed an "Act of God" by courts, absolving the brewery of liability.

4. **The Pope's Astronomer** - The Vatican has its observatory and even an appointed astronomer! This position, dating back to the 16th century, highlights the Catholic Church's complex relationship with science, navigating between faith and the stars.

5. **Religious Robots** - In Japan, a Buddhist temple uses a robotic priest to deliver sermons. This modern approach aims to engage a tech-savvy generation, blending ancient traditions with futuristic technology.

6. **Flying Monks** - Legend states that medieval Irish monks believed they could reach paradise by sailing west. St. Brendan supposedly made such a voyage, inspiring centuries of explorers who believed in a mystical land across the Atlantic.

7. **Jediism**—Inspired by the Star Wars films, Jediism has been recognized as an official religion in several countries. Followers believe the Force is a binding, metaphysical power, proving that pop culture can spawn genuine spiritual movements.

8. **The Whistling God** - Among the Zapotec people of Mexico, the deity Cocijo is believed to control rain and lightning, often depicted as whistling to summon the storm clouds—an ancient form of weather forecasting!

9. **Vegetarian Gods** - In Hinduism, the deity Ganesha is said to have a sweet tooth, particularly for modaks, sweet dumplings. Temples often offer these treats to the deity during worship, catering to divine

preferences.

10. **Sacred Surfing** - In ancient Hawaii, surfing was not just a sport but a religious ritual. Chiefs and commoners rode the waves to appease the sea gods, a divine session on the ocean's swells.

11. **Holy Hat Policy** - The Jewish Kippah and the Sikh turban share a common purpose: they are worn to show reverence and humility before God, covering the head as a sign of respect in their respective religious practices.

12. **Gospel of the Pews** - A church in the Netherlands offers a "Lazy Church" service where congregants can attend worship in their pajamas. This service is designed for relaxation and spiritual rejuvenation, emphasizing comfort in seeking closeness with God.

13. **Zombie Saints** - The Middle Ages were rife with tales of saints who returned from the dead to lead the faithful or deliver messages from beyond. These stories illustrated medieval Christian folklore's blurred lines between life, death, and sainthood.

14. **Divine Accidents** - Historical records from the Byzantine Empire tell of a church that was struck by lightning shortly after its consecration—a sign some interpret as divine displeasure. In contrast, others saw it as a mere natural occurrence.

15. **The Sacred Coconut** - In certain parts of India, coconuts are used in Hindu rituals to symbolize the breaking of the ego to reveal the purity within, a spiritual smash hit during various ceremonies.

16. **Blessed Be the Pets** - Many churches worldwide

conduct annual pet blessing ceremonies, where animals of all shapes and sizes receive blessings from the clergy, acknowledging their role in humans' spiritual lives.

17. **The Laughing Buddha** - Contrary to popular belief, the Laughing Buddha is not the founder of Buddhism, Siddhartha Gautama, but a Chinese monk who lived centuries later and became a symbol of contentment and abundance.

18. **Nun-Such Park** - In England, a park known as Nun's Island where, according to legend, mischievous spirits of former nuns wander, said to have been nuns who broke their solemn vows.

19. **Singing Stones** - At certain Tibetan monasteries, monks use large stones in rituals believed to 'sing' when struck in a particular way, creating a chant-like resonance considered a voice from the heavens.

20. **Heavenly Insurance** - Some medieval churches had lightning rods disguised as crosses, an early form of 'divine' insurance against storm damage, marrying practicality with piety.

1. **Monotheistic Beliefs**: A significant number of the world's religions are monotheistic, which means adherents believe in the existence of one supreme God. Prominent examples include Christianity, Islam, and Judaism. Each of these religions refers to its deity as the one and only true God and often incorporates this belief as a central doctrine of faith.

2. **Hafiz Count**: It is estimated that millions of Muslims have committed the entire Quran to memory. These

individuals are known as Hafiz or Hafiza. The practice of memorizing the Quran is particularly revered in the Muslim world, with schools and institutions dedicated to memorization across Islamic countries.

3. **Religious Manuscripts**: The Dead Sea Scrolls, some of the oldest known Christian and Jewish biblical manuscripts, date between the 3rd century BCE and the 1st century CE. These texts include some of the only copies of certain biblical books before the 2nd century AD.

Also by Michael P. Clutton

Secrets of a Reluctant Genius
Weight Loss Without Dieting

Your Great Big Grab Bag of Useless Helpful Tidbits
Religions of the World

Watch for more at www.michaelpclutton.com.

About the Author

Michael P. Clutton isn't your typical storyteller. Since he was young, he loved drawing cartoons and writing stories, which not only kept him busy but also helped him learn more words. This early passion for fiction laid the foundation for his unique voice—rich, imaginative, and brimming with wit.

Michael's sarcastic and unique perspective on life adds intrigue to his daily routine and captivates those around him. Known for his quick wit and self-deprecating humor, he can generate a giggle or a guffaw at the drop of a hat. His creative toolbox is well-stocked with both artwork and the written word, making him a versatile and dynamic creator.

Michael and his wife live in peaceful Southwest Florida, where they find inspiration in the beautiful surroundings. Whether he's playing poker, fishing, or crafting unique digital art, his creativity knows no bounds. Even as he ages, his commitment to expressing creativity through writing and artwork remains strong.

Michael's two adult children have inherited his creativity and are carrying on his cherished artistic legacy. His work invites readers into a world of creative imagination, where each story and piece of art is a testament to his lifelong passion for the craft.

Discover the captivating world of Michael P. Clutton, an author who combines humor, heart, and a deep passion for creativity in his stories and art.

Read more at www.michaelpclutton.com.